.

A Cage in Search of a Bird

poems by

Kathleen Holliday

Finishing Line Press
Georgetown, Kentucky

A Cage in Search of a Bird

ACKNOWLEDGMENTS

Grateful acknowledgment to the editors and judges of the following
publications and contests in which these poems first appeared or placed.

Cathexis Northwest Press: "When Asked if She Regretted"
Common Ground Review Poetry Contest 2022: "Running in the Dark" (first
prize, judge Abby E. Murray)
Fish Publishing Poetry Prize 2022: "A Cage in Search of a Bird," (long-listed,
judge Billy Collins)
Ponder Review: "Learning to Swim"
Shark Reef Literary Magazine: "After Dinner, Atlantis" "August"
The Write Launch: "My Near-Death Experience"

IN GRATITUDE

My heartfelt thanks to the Women Writers of the Salish Sea: Suzanne Berry,
Brooks, Marty Clark, Iris Graville, Rita Larom Hoffman, Lorna Reese and
Gretchen Wing for their continued guidance, insight and generosity. I am
honored to be in the company of such literary citizens. And to Susie Teague,
gifted herbalist and healer.

Publisher: Leah Huete de Maines
Editor: Christen Kincaid
Cover Art: Great Blue Heron, Santa Cruz Island, Galapagos, ©iStock.com/
SL—Photography
Author Photo: Robert S. Harrison
Cover Design: Elizabeth Maines McCleavy

Order online: www.finishinglinepress.com
also available on amazon.com

Author inquiries and mail orders:
Finishing Line Press
PO Box 1626
Georgetown, Kentucky 40324
USA

Contents

In memory
of
my brother
Michael Thomas Holliday
another cage
in search of a bird

.

A Cage in Search of a Bird

I am a cage, in search of a bird.
Franz Kafka

So much depends upon
a little hinged door
held open:

where sometimes a canary
consoling itself with song
swings

sometimes an upstart crow
raucous, an iridescent sheen
preens

sometimes a mourning dove
head under a wing
grieves

more often a shade
taloned, rapt, amber-eyed
broods

a beating of air
a tearing of flesh
sometimes even in my sleep.

Learning to Swim

I begin the day
sitting on the edge of the bed
uncertain, before launching
myself into the shallows.

I move through the day
breasting waves
toeing for certainty
swaying like kelp.

More often, letting go,
giving in to buoyancy
I move through the day
where all I take with me
is a memory of shore.

Sunlight Pours into the House

Spilling into the brass bowl,
burnishing the pale wall gold.

The topography of plaster
now a page of cuneiform
I cannot read,

my fingertips trace the light.
My body blooms.

Unlike Albert Camus

After 22 winters in Minnesota
I discovered there was not
in me an invincible summer.

The Fifth Month of Winter

March. Minneapolis. Snow again.
This blizzard triggers an avalanche,
and buries all hope of spring.

At the convenience store,
losing a tug o' war
for the last 4-pack of toilet paper
I settle for cigarettes and
hurry home, bent to the cold.

Kneeling, as if pleading would
appease the force of the wind,
my gloved hands fumble at the door
like an astronaut on the dark
side of the moon.

Before the key turns,
a dog whimpers desperate
to be let back in.
I stamp my feet free of snow
and galumph up the stairs.

Once an icepack of frozen
breaths—my scarf
sizzles on the radiator.

There's no place but home
on a night like this –
nothing new to read,
no room to pace,
I flop back and forth,
a rabbit in its hutch.

My little tv flickers to life—
The Wizard of Oz.

The tornado swallows everything
in its path. Dorothy's house spins
around and around then drops down
into Oz with a thud.

When she opens the door, I recall
I saw this film a dozen times in black
and white before seeing it in color.

All I think on this night is:
all those players
who portrayed Dorothy,
the Scarecrow,
the Tin Man,
the Cowardly Lion,
the Wicked Witch of the West,
the Great Oz Himself,
all those Munchkins,
are dead now,
and Toto too.

A Walk in the Woods

Years ago, I quit smoking,
yet here, on this leafy wooded trail,
striding along in the dappled green light,
reverting to my natural state,
I shuffle to a halt.

Bending low to tie my shoes,
I rise up on my haunches—
Ursa Major, standing tall,
shaggy paws raised,
head nodding up and up
to catch the scent of a Camel Light
on the wind.

Native Tongue
(from *Sonnets from the Felinese)*

Though he's been dead these many years,
last night I dreamt of my cat.

He spoke to me—not in English
which he learned for my sake,
though to be truthful, in all his lives
he could not speak it, only read it.

He spoke, rather, in his own
delicate pink tongue,
an idiom of the present tense:

My bowl is full,
my body warm in the sun,
my sky full of birds.

He turned from the window.
At last, he said, *you understand.*

Nocturne

Awake and wondering

is there an island in the ocean
its pale-green translucent reef
the accretion of all my disposable
contact lenses,

and does it stare back
at the moon?

Echo

Turn onto your left side
the technician says
as I lie down in a hollow space
on the table.

Breathe in. Stop.
And I slip away.

How easy it is to return
to the water.

Breathe slow. Deep.

She touches the screen
plays back tiny bits,
the sounds of my heart;

a murmur, odd, yet so familiar,
breaking the surface
then submerged,

like whale song,
interrupted.

Reading Poetry During a Power Outage

One moment standing up in the living room,
the next, fallen down a mine shaft,
blinkered by darkness. Slowly, arms windmilling,
I bluff the miles to the kitchen countertop.

After a dark age, my fingers feel for, hold fast
a flashlight I balance on the arm of the sofa.
A book now held open in my hands,
the light falls just so, an illuminated page.

Parallel lines flare—the tunneling
of those who have gone before.
In that blazing reveal, in the contours
of syllables, other voices call out,

I begin to feel sure of the way shown
by those light-bearers, word-wielders, deep-delvers.
There's no need then to fear; those ahead
have set the darkness echoing.

Rounded with a Sleep

When we finally
lay our heads down
on the earth

will we be like children
facing each other shyly
listening for a soothing voice?

Rest now.
When you wake
it will be Storytime.
And after that,
Art and Music.

His and Hers
(Eleanor of Aquitaine and Henry II)

In separate tombs Eleanor and Henry lie
in the crypt of the Abbey of Fontevrault.
They've been here awhile.

When they wed in that year 1152,
there was no mistaking his towels
for hers in the royal garderobe:
the flaming lion rampant on red,
the fleur-de-lis of blue on gold.

And when they lay side by side
in that marriage bed, England
and the Angevin lands united,
they pulled their joint demesne
up to their chins, like a pieced quilt.

When the abbey's iron-studded doors
creak shut, and all the tourists have gone,
they're left to themselves again.
As the shadows of ten centuries fall
from the vaulted ceiling,
his hand steals across the narrow
aisle between them, still lusting
after what remains of her huge tracts of land—
this oblong niche where she's interred.

She slaps his hand away,
adjusts her golden circlet
more comfortably on her head,
smooths the stony folds of her gown,
resumes her prayerbook reading;
in her repose, the tracery of a smile.

For she, queen consort, Duchess of Aquitaine,
lived long after her second husband,
and his turbulent priest.

Her Henry, with all his titles,
once a King of England, was born in Le Mans,
and lies next to her,
within a roped-off square of space,
in France.

The Shape of Water/
An Empath in Love

A
cup
of broth hot
held in two hands.
A heated swimming
pool steaming. A tidal
pool braced for the
next wave. The dark
depths where the
Titanic lies.

My Near-Death Experience

If I loved you,
being this close would kill me.
Dorianne Laux

As near-death experiences go,
it was one of the best.
What more is there to tell?

How to explain then the wandering
alone in the Underworld, knowing
he would not be back.

How they came from every circle,
spirits out of the shadows,

all of us there, even there,
drawn to the music.

The Final Problem

Like Holmes regretting
the absence of Moriarty,
tonight, (just tonight, you see)
I think of my enemy so arch,
that Casanova of crime,
our *crime passionnel,*

the great pounding
of water above our heads
that moment two protagonists
locked in embrace

plummet into the roar
over the Reichenbach
of our own imagination.

How far we fell.

And as we fell,
were our eyes
closed or open?

Divorce,
a haiku

That cold day we flew
leaving him there on the ground.
None of us waving.

When Asked if She Regretted

When asked if she regretted not
marrying again, my mother said,
No, though it would have been nice
to go out to dinner once in a while.

Her never-married daughter,
how I've lingered over wine lists,
forsaken all others but one on the
fold-out pages,

not always resisting the temptation
of dessert, how often I've regretted
the handing back of the menu.

Though No One Told Us

Though no one told us
of our long-estranged father's death
somehow we knew.

How startling, to find ourselves
bobbing up out of the ocean
in sight of shore, gasping
great gulps of air.

A quick head count.
One of us raised the question.
Another shook their head.

We used to be afraid of the water.
On that day, we remembered why.

If My Father Could Ask Why I Have Tattoos

So I could be inscribed,
imprinted, a broadsheet
layered over my skin
this copy one of one.

So my body could show:
I've crossed more seas
than you.

I made it back to shore
you son of a bitch.

August

for my siblings

As if drought could ever empty it
the well of grief glimmers full
topped up like a bitter drink
we never ordered.

That last August on the farm
the water level in the well so low
we dipped buckets down
into the galvanized tank
beaded silver like sweat.

As if we could ever carry enough
water back to that house on fire.

Hemispheres

And I dreamt of two
walnut shells

how the halves
fit together

as if they'd never been
pulled apart
and emptied.

After Dinner, Atlantis

A dishwater dam,
this foaming reservoir.

Every knife, fork, and spoon,
every dinner plate drowned.

A wine glass sinks, tolling,
an undersea village bell.

The Green and the Blue

Never the eagle
always the rabbit.

Ever this low green
world, and then,

So much blue—
And the view!

Running in the Dark

A sharp thump in the night
against the house. I think,
windfall, and go back to reading,

But in the daylight, a deer,
a yearling, running in the dark.
Dead.

I grip two legs and
drag the cold, stiff body
to an open space between trees,

marvel at every shade of brown,
the soft tufted ears, catch my breath
at the bent neck.

A skyful of wing shadow
circling and circling
comes down and covers it.

And then, all that's left:
a flap of hide, a broken cage
of bones, black hooves like empty shoes.

A running away from
or a running to?

A Worthy Adversary

Bare feet
and white pajamas,
my palms pressed together,
I bow.

When sensei says,
"First step, Little House Cat,
select a worthy adversary,"

I glance around the room
and choose myself.

Rafting

On this wide dark sea
let us do as otters do.
Here, take this hand, this paw.

We'll rise and slowly turn
on the night's tide
and not let go.

And not let go.

Born in the Pacific Northwest, **Kathleen Holliday** has lived most of her life there and in the Midwest. As a teenager, she emigrated with her family to Australia and then to Minnesota where she spent 22 winters before returning home to Washington State.

A graduate of Augsburg University and former library staffer with a passion for words, Kathleen's poems have appeared in many literary journals including *Cathexis Northwest Press*, *Common Ground Review*, *Poet Lore*, *Poetry Super Highway*, *SHARK REEF Literary Magazine*, and *The Write Launch*. Her previous chapbooks, *Putting My Ash on the Line*, and *Boatman, Pass By* were also published by Finishing Line Press.

After decades of urban life, Kathleen is grateful to call an island in the San Juan Archipelago in Washington State—one of many unceded ancestral lands of the Coast Salish people—home.